The Old Man Who Swam Away and Left Only His Wet Feet

The Old Man
Who Swam Away
and Left Only His Wet Feet

Gene Frumkin

LA ALAMEDA PRESS • ALBUQUERQUE

ACKNOWLEDGEMENTS

Since this collection spans almost three decades, I have many people to thank for help and guidance through the years, although I can't hope to have gotten all their names into these lists.

First is my mentor back at the old Los Angeles State College, the late Thomas McGrath, a superb teacher whose work and integrity were a model for many of us, his students and friends.

For their active assistance in seeing my work into print, I must thank Michael Anania, Jon Gill Bentley, Gus Blaisdell, the late Patrick Bowles, Jeff and Cirrelda Snider-Bryan, Bobby and Lee Byrd, Glenna Luschei, the late Rob Cuscaden, Ron Offen, the late Alan Swallow, the late E.W. Tedlock, Jr., and Paul Vangelisti.

To those who have read my work and offered valuable, sometimes tough criticism, as well as always-needed morale boosting, I am much indebted: David Abel, Rudolfo and Patricia Anaya, Lee Bartlett, Mei-mei Berssenbrugge, Alvaro Cardona-Hine, Robert Creeley, Sharon Di Maria, Clayton Eshleman, William Fox, Phillip Foss, Sid Gershgoren, Keith Gunderson, Joy Harjo, George Hitchcock, David Johnson, Milton Kessler, Stanley Kiesel, Nathaniel Mackey, Tony Mares, Barbara McCauley, Michael McClure, Karen McKinnon, the late Bert Meyers, Sheila Murphy, Estelle Gershgoren Novak, Stanley Noyes, Robert Peterson, Janet Rodney, Jeanne Shannon, Ron Silliman, Frank Stewart, Arthur Sze, Nathaniel Tarn, David Till, John Tritica, the late John Unterecker, Mark Vinz, and Keith and Heloise Wilson.

Finally I wish to heap many gratitudes on two friends, Mary Rising Higgins and Mel Weisburd, who have read my work and critiqued it through conversations, the mails, and by phone with what I can only feel as devotion beyond the call.

Dostoevsky & Other Nature Poems was originally published by Solo Press (San Luis Obispo, 1972).
It was reprinted in full in *Manoa,* Vol. 1, Nos. 1 & 2 (double issue).
A Lover's Quarrel With America was originally published by Automatic Press (Albuquerque, 1985).
"Rilke's Razor, Jung's Version," was presented orally at the art exhibition *Inescapable Histories: Mel Chin*, sponsored by the Scottsdale for the Arts Cultural Council as part of its Poetry Series.

Cover painting:: Scott Greene—"Whirlpool" 24 x 30 in. (oil on linen) 1997
Frontis drawing:: Lydia Samuels Frumkin (1938-1981)—"Two Birds" (ink on paper) 1961

ISBN:: 1-888809-08-6
Library of Congress Number:: 97-078139

La Alameda Press
9636 Guadalupe Trail NW
Albuquerque, New Mexico 87114

to *Ali and Danny*
with all love

CONTENTS

Dostoevsky and Other Nature Poems

A Lover's Quarrel with America

THE RENATURING CYCLE

A GOOD STORY

New Poems

Dostoevsky
& Other Nature Poems
1972

THE PERFECTION OF SUMMER THUNDERSHOWERS

Every afternoon around 4 o'clock the leaves discover a wind
behind the wind a thunderhead emerges from its hiding-place
The rain pellets the heat's thick plate

                                          Afterward, an hour at most
                a few puddles have grown
                blue green gold and red
                      in a few rutty beds
                    in alleys   on the streets
                          in craters of grass
        The heat surrounds the puddles
they form concentric cycles

                              You as a man within your shelter
watched the preparation for the rain then the rain itself
For a brief time
              while it rained
                    you were happy
The world you live in had changed for the better
                            You, a critical man
                had been the rain
           as you had been the heat

            The rain was perfect and you had lived perfectly
since nothing could have been preferred
                      to the rain
        As a critical man
                at the height of the downpour

(though still a nameless well-concealed lodger)

a flaw

had already found a warm spot in your heart

Not that the rain would stop
but that it was perfect

ALBUQUERQUE SPLEEN

On warm nights in late June   at 2 a.m. on warm nights
                as you lead the full Albuquerque moon
                                                by a leash
the future leaks into your shoes
                                        Your feet are wet
                                                the streets are warm and dry
There is the moon 'not the white moon of idylls which resembles
a frigid bride' but your own moon with its sound of a single cymbal
brash against the warm air
                                You have read Baudelaire and agree
                        that Time doesn't fly
                                        but is a slow flea in Mistress Earth's
                                                perfect ambush
So you flee   Your feet are drunk
                                        tomorrow is already today
You tip the moon   it's a wobbling saucer   it barks at you
                                                        at your feet
                                                so porous
                        the wine rising warming legs and thighs
You believe on those warm nights this elixir is the future
                                        and that it doesn't exist
                        It's all in your feet
                        All you're doing is going

WAITING FOR GODOT IN CLASS

So I stood there and said 'As I say this the present is already the past'
later stood in the classroom corner   moved back to the lectern   'Where I
                                                     stood before
is now the past   where I stand now is the present'   Time in motion
from space to space
                             But I can't stand at the lectern forever
            Beckett would never forgive me
                                     So the prospect
                         of the next step
                 in time
                       which is the future
I don't know if they who watched me
                       are still waiting for something to happen

The sky has shifted several times today but at no time have I observed
that silvery blue sky above a park in Newark at which I am present again
at felicitous moments   for a few seconds   now and then
               a merging of all my times from childhood to possible old age
Such a sky I said to them
                     is more profound to me
                              than a signed contract
                  I still don't know what I meant
           other than the meaning
which demands no promises
                      That same sky may favor me again
                 I won't watch for it
                     nor impossibly move toward it

My next step was to say 'The class has concluded   I have
                   nothing more to say until tomorrow'

THE MASK (MASQUE) OF MARCEL DUCHAMP

The Nude has descended the staircase   where the carpeted floor
   is absent   there is only a face in the wind
                                 a device
                engineered to cover the void of ground
to entice the Nude from her bedroom
                        There is wind
        and a face grinding its teeth
                    where She would stand
           under normal skies
The Nude flies downward
           nowhere else to go no other mind
               to go there

She should have stayed upstairs   in her bedroom   have given
her bodies to faceless paramours
                  should have screwed on all fours
      It's all the same though   a game
Because of the abyss downstairs there is no guarantee of a place upstairs
where a Nude could hang her clothes on   there is no reason to suppose
the wind is softer there than anywhere
               Around the staircase
      is purely air

     The face below is also above
grinning at the merest mechanics of love
             With its malleable its tortured smile
    with precise invisible hands
          it probably gave
     the Nude one final shove

HYPNOS WAKING KNOCKS AT THE DOOR

Candle of the dozen woods
                              another year flattens its face against the glass
            Reading the poems of René Char
                                        what is there
                        you do not understand?
                                              Simply the rhetoric
                                        of this very question
                  As the small blaze of each arrival
snuffs itself out in your house
                                    what amazement each hour invites
                  how short your breath
                  how long a distance to the next survival
And that is how you receive your guests
                                          with a longing   not to be
            trampled by the shy poems of their love

THE MOTH

As Your hand holds the feverish moth
        what glow of energy compels its wings to strike
           with all their strength
        out of their darkness

The Amazon   a drop of sweat on Your brow
        oceans trickle through Your fingers as You refresh Yourself
        in the morning of every millennium

              Our planet is a blue apple
         in Your orchard   The zephyrs roam through space
               gently shaking the stars
                    that are all plums and apricots

              Your hand releases its captive
the moth flies freely toward its own enlightenment
                 and its own good night

These words are my first to love Your absence God
and I shall never diminish You with praise again
                You Who are perfect
         Who have opened Your hand
      and allowed all the power there is
                   to lose itself
        among Earth's creatures
    we who still   foolishly
        cluster about its radiance

THE PROCESSION

On a white anthill
spring's first iris

How does an iris love?
With its thin curling ears
with its purple drooping ears
The Chinese elm in the yard is dying
on warped crutches
How does it die?
On a mound of leprosy
a fever of the skin
The sun goes down leaving a bitter aftertaste
it has fallen away
the air a dull blue aftermath
You had expected much today
from this carnal fruit superbly conditioned to endure
How will the sun manage to climb again to arrive at noon again
while you sit on a pile of frozen snow
dozing
dreaming of one more warmth?

Tomorrow you reach out
something reluctant scrapes your fingers
it tastes like red hair
it is almost visible / a white grain of sand in a red anthill
It sticks in your eye until you see finally a crystalline female form
and go blind with love

or will drown in the socket?
You are as foolish as the sun

THE NATURE OF MY SEXUAL PROBLEM

                                        Wind, you are a member
                        of my body
                                the breath itself

Mountains, you are my face
                        Rivers, my blood
                        Earth, my skin
                        Sun, you are my eyes
Without the thunder I cannot hear
Without the doorknob there is nothing to touch
                        The savor of rainbows is in my mouth
        There is nothing outside of me that is not within me

I travel day after day across the world
                                        to open one woman's eyelids
                        When she sees me
        I see myself
Then dream myself to sleep again   back in my hovel

                        Always the feathers of some woman's love
                drifting drifting
                                through the sky
                                        which is my heart
I see myself continually reaching for one blue feather
                                        to kiss it forever
        The sky so huge, my heart so small

STILL LIFE WITH PEAR AND OLD MAN

For the absence of love, a slightly rouged pear
An old man lies in wait for you
                  he is there in the penny arcade
cranking a vintage burlesque show
he is wild as 10 peyote buttons
                      his head's an opera of sex
          soprano and basso profundo in one
If you offer him a bottle of whale oil
       will he accept it gratefully?

                     You think you will retrace your steps
Somewhere there must be that Mexican plaza where your daughter in her stroller
held a red balloon in her hand
                Your wife was wheeling the stroller
You hadn't thought of bottled memory then   the old man too
                      was so far in the background
          you couldn't see him with a microscope

Your wife still loves you in her LA letters
Those faded mirrors: you look like the Sandia Mountains 10 minutes after
      they have outgrown the big orange balloon
Such times are the settling wings of an eagle   such silence is friendly
      and absence the applause of the universe
Send a bouquet to anyone
                  while the old geezer gets dizzy
         riding his ambush
             outside the moment's limits

Dawn Vision: Hot & Cool

                                                          A few bones
                                                    a few stones
                        Rio Grande dry again
        avenue of mud through the middle of Albuquerque
                        sky immured
                                              in its rented cradle
An Indian has opened his Mexican eyes   it is morning
                                                    a green vehicle drifts
                    in the distance   in dilatory passage via a frontage road
            Burnt-out wind
                                      a few bones
                        a few stones
The mind is an anvil the blows are heavy   Black Indian bronze Jew
                                                    no others will do
Four years rocking to and fro across the dead duke's city
                                    and still the deep maroon chiles
                    dangling in clusters by doorways
        are creatures of a song
                        whose seeds are bitter
                                              are strong
        Slag-black earth
                        the orchards are few
        The mind is a fragment of desert
where all detritus is baked anew
                        Always the Jew's Mosaic daydream in a clay or stone
                the blue-skinned messenger is on his way

FRIDAY AFTERNOON MAY 29 1970

In this late afternoon of a quiet village the sun barely resembles
Van Gogh   Hard to believe the devil dwells there

                  smoking

        his red cigar

the smoke-rings demolishing entire theologies

              He is there though

        we dare not be deceived

                  It is his fire

        devours the elm leaves

and penetrates the closed eyelids with an orange potion
so we are tempted to sleep as if deep in the belly of love

Van Gogh saw him saw Blake's angels

              contorted squirming

        long worms and small ones in the blazing pit

a pot of stewing entrails amazed by their own beauty
within the motion of their tortured days in heaven

            on earth

Almost evening

    the gnats that dance above the grass

    stay in the dodging sunlight as long as they can

DOSTOEVSKY

When the river shines
     those nights of green translucent bones
the bearded man fishes for stars   He groans in this labor
which takes all his strength   What is hidden beneath the waters:
     a substance of moths
          The stars slip away
     steadfastly
          no hook of light so pure
     it can hold fast to the steady flow
The man's eyes / ecstatic beams
     fasten onto the golden mean of transmutation
     To still the slippery bones
it is the tongue he must use   no other weapon burns with such energy
Sweating he sips the river   green smoke tears into his eyes
Night after night he fishes for stars
     his tongue a coal a small orange curve among
the gleaming green darts that resist in darkness
     and still resist
until at last and then again he catches one

     It is a secret he cannot part from
     who spent his life learning it
The bones of the river are his stars
     they are ashes in his brain
He is the icon the cauldron to whom we kneel in our bones
beloved God beloved original of sin
     who knows how to stab himself to the heart
     with his baited crosier

Proust Pro Naturam

Of you who withheld yourself in your later years
from the imprecisions of health   who clung spiderlike to your soundless room
        at 102 Boulevard Haussmann
                breathing through gauze   fighting the war
                        against life as you fought it against death
                of you Marcel I write most surely
in this installment on nature

                        Your allergy to flowers to all fragrances
                your surreal asthma
        the stony requiem of your Time Regained
lead me precisely toward the groping delusions of my dying elms
as they stand in sunlight   and my stand for years there, chalky-faced
                leaves returning season after season
        my elms lovely in dying

You Marcel, 50 years without a word, return to me
sickly in passion, fawning like Rilke in your letters, a liar
                in all the truth you knew by heart

        How pleasant never to have known you
so I can admire the music of your wheezing lungs
in the long weaving sentences you wrote
                in the same breath as I observed yesterday
                the golden-breasted bird who glided from branch to branch
in my elms   then swooped down to stutter in the grass
                its brief, almost personal, salutation
before it flew out of sight

A Lover's Quarrel With America
1985

I
THE RENATURING CYCLE

THE RENATURING CYCLE

Dreaming is the psyche itself
doing its soul-work
—James Hillman

Slowly the axe grows crazy in catalpa wood
                    slowly the bole grows out of itself
            out of earth
                                it narrows down from simple standing
                                        into a bent sleep
The axe is brilliant in the shadows   a blade streaking silver through mottles of sun
it is action   a fierce energy   merciless
                                                though later
                the axe will also tip against plankwall
            no light entering then its place of depth
and there   leaning into sleep   will be helpless as dried and sullied seaweed
A thing   this tested instrument   alone unto its acts
                                            undergrown by older life
                            back then ages back
                that blackmoon country

                            The tree roots itself in virginal sky
                            a capsized umbrella
whose shade is white and warming   a warning, axe:
                                            the undertow of objects
                (like the human night-soul)   pulls counter the tides
                Everything survives in the negative
The day forgets

SCRIPT

Miracle of the worm
permutation out of earth into
syllables
lines of thought vocable as trails of semen in the dust
worm who struggles from silence with deliberate gymnastics
to erupt in time as the marvelous snake

seducer of woman
corrupter of man
through a speech so concealed in the flora of its consonance
so elusive in desire
that the grasping brain could not construe the physical de-formation of its blueprint
that very one it laid out on wild grass with ancient subtlety
saying: "Here is the world"

Earthworm, superb syllabus of intellect
one wriggle in the twitch of an eyelid
you will never open your magisterial heart to butterflies hairsprays colorblindness
and such creatures of mind as Freud and the Surrealist Manifestos
all of which exist through human sympathy   objectively
as bodies in the human environment

We must believe, worm of tongues
ambassador of divine monarchy

that footnote
which encloses all the stories ever given voice
for a script of intercourse
consummated only in your sucking mouth where the end is endlessly secreted

September Evening

for Floyce Alexander

No more talk on the patio
   September a dry blue refulgence clings to the sky over the mesas
         clings to the sky we remember
as the friend of all our years always blue always the awakener
Our talk diverged from what our lives were now
           although in the darkening blue
       the sky maintained its moment alive for us
    I don't want to leave
         never again leave the finished history
of this calm somewhat sanguine witness to all our digressions
Sorrowful brothers
      let us not refuse even one resurgent moment
   and wherever it is we must go after this evening
I trust the calendar that rips mythology from its numbers
I trust the caves which no one has entered
I trust the unblossomed heaven the sere petals of its angels
I want to see one more breach like this one more opening
         to silence
    absence written in sunblooded leaves of aspen birch and yew
leaves ready to fall slip away into hollowing light
       Brothers the moon absorbs us gently
   all circles must end

Arbitrary Design

Hickory nuts lie smashed in fallen powdered leaves
Someone is preparing a charm
                        will sprinkle on gooseberries
                        phlox and sauce of papaya
                        Galapagos-egg saltspray grass of sorrow
            then stir until ready to cook
"A foolish arbitrary design":
                              the wind carries these words to me
    in caravans of snow   everything has shifted from long ago
extensions, a traveling
            That's fine
                        When one is ravenous for love
    even the corpse of snow
                  inspires an embrace
                              and one moment for the teeth to flare
flare out, dying
                  matchboxes
                              sucked into the stars
        our crushed and mangled stars

'Something'

We want this to be about "something"
      a fact if possible
      or at least
                           a simulation
            detachable
like an organ   from the spherical music
                             from the supernal flesh
It's how one says it
          the system
                  where we live
          our crowded intestines
     reels of film entangled, cutting into one   another
                  no longer separable
        as images

      Why then prolong this terminal discourse
about "something"?
                  It is enough to assent
      that heaven is androgynous
and we are issues formed in time
                 dyadic and processional
       Drapes around a nude figure
    in stone or air

BAD AIR IMPRISONED IN THE VENTILATING SYSTEM

Scorpius, the nailed whip of wisdom belongs in that home designed by the father
                                                              of skyscrapers
house devoured by glass overlooking any city its mystical lights collected
                                                  in the nightwindow's frame
            structure of devotion, shifting in earth.   How to believe,
                                                              Scorpius
                  in so fragile a demonstration of mankind's power
                  Poison is everywhere   prepared to scourge the flesh of natural
                                                              humor
and those who do not move their furniture into stylish pent-up houses where
                                          god is tailor-made
Selfish prayers rise in air   vaporous towers
                                    glass needles stalk the veins of our sky
                  Robert Chetkin died a year ago
                                    another OD come to light on the same day Jean
                                                              Seberg
            was found in her white Paris Renault 10 days in the devil's arms
skull & bones actress   staked and burned by Quaker Nixon's secret agents
            while Chetkin poet of disillusioned air
            former student, arm wrestler   said to have been lonely
            mixed his wine with too many spiked wafers   unmarked in
                                                  passing   like
or not Mayakovsky Lenny Bruce many others whose names are closed to reporters
                                                              and the times

                  Your glass house Chet
            (round bespectacled face black hair a compact gentle man)
as well as Saint Jean Seberg's   also that punk rock slayer's   all self-stung
                                                              Scorpius,

toxic fingernails and gondolas of black semen beleaguer all
our vows
prayers are closets where dead bodies hang
Why lonely Chet?   Why not lifeparties and walks through
jewflower gardens?
Why not a snow of blue and incredibly fleecy bells?

As you said
"nothing survives in the temperate zone"
Scorpius oversees the museum of stars   the church of broken glass scattered
across the heavens

The Hallway

Between here and there
this hallway vanishes
behind one
with each step
taken

Arrival then is from nowhere
as if one interviewed Kaiser Wilhelm II
after the final defeat of his generals at the Marne
"Was that it   a river?   and therein my soldiers lie
washing back to some untraceable source?"
But the kaiser also is mysteriously not present
reportedly dead since 1941
a hard man to corner if one is a journalist and needs
just this particular interview for a raise or promotion
Better perhaps not to arrive   to pause in the hallway
between this and that
Let the soldiers die in peace   the River Marne runs colder now
and alters its course slightly
to accommodate history
There is no logos (so long after the lackword
of a beginning)
but what the hand inscribes and
thought erases from the child's blackboard

THE EPILEPTICS

One who has done hard work
One who waits many hours
One who smokes and shouldn't
Another who finishes every crossword puzzle
Ourselves in cynical ecstasy
what can we say to people
who live their lives outside
the pen that describes our circle?
But we shouldn't end
on a question   a thankless thought
you and I elusive in each other's arms

One who gets married
One who grows in trees
and these others whose edges are lapped by the seas
into polished architraves
No,
let us believe serenely in laughter
the laughter of our selves
who devour our own /
each other's
tongues

THE AGE NOW ENDING

So the Romantic Age ends
                    as it crawled through the mirror of brutal water
          crawled headfirst   body severed from its caul to the navel of statues
                    that have stood all night in the cold
                                        bearing starfrost with stoic and inhuman calm

          The Age now ending questioned the heart
as if it were water   and the heart answered clawing like a lobster boiled alive
How cunning the crustacean's quiet agony
                              for to speak aloud in such condition
                    would be to tear the cloth which conceals our tattered set
              all the actors caught gazing long into their armored glass

          So this Age is a vision of melodrama
in which death is not tragic and sin lives grandly enough in a Las Vegas hotel
For those of us who cannot buy the heart's conscious cross
              there lies the sea in its blue cape
                    the carnal sea
                                        We stare out across it
                    toward its cessation
              where we accept the mind's provisional line
marking us off as marginal creatures
                              concentrated into one horizon

2
A GOOD STORY

A Figure of Immutable Force

He sits outside on the olivegreen earth
                knees tucked under   hands flat on his thighs
                        an impossible position
                                      it seems
                    to sustain
                           Yet his head
small above the huge hard chunk of body
        has fallen to his chest in sleep
                Elemental visage the same harsh heavy blue
            as the sky's   lost between maroon dusk
                    and water's evening indigo
Overhead a scrap of cloud
            illuminates his dream like an interior moon
        He has held his place here
                  from the beginning   embraced by stone
Massive power moves through him
        this dozing monument
                          immune from desire
        whose image precedes all words

THE DANDY

This dapper morning reflects a sudden belief in
imitation as it walks with sharp strides
                    into the musky scent of the boulevard's aftershave lotion
                         This morning witnesses
            nothing original in the shape of an apple
and nothing premeditated in a man's brisk legs
        when they discover emergencies under brimming leaves

            Copies of death lurk at every corner
                    of this morning   in every art shop and Safeway
                            in the famous cathedrals of France
                and brothels of Corpus Christi
    Only tall humidity stands against
the wordy dandy who so charmingly confronts his image in glass
        imagines himself a crisp lettuce
                a world that corresponds with amusing
                            parables outside his clearly marked Exit
        What wilts is the morning's muse on stilts

                        And then coming back
            wearing the veil of dusk
        who would remember the gifted clothing the grooming
this very day's origin?
        Time's petrified scrawl signifies a repetition
                which defies all exotic departures
            bundles them away in burlap sacks that trucks pick up
and take somewhere
        Tomorrow gets up groggy   knowing it remains yesterday
It gets dressed   white spats and an amber bamboo cane

strolls jauntily into itself

                    and waits at the corner for the light to change
             for the light seductive
       O great swine O green eye boiling in the dreamlocked crater

SEDIMENTS

When he glares at his reflection
opens his maw in a huge black yowl
    he comments on the accretion of moments of instants
      and what it leaves in sediments
        what is not expelled
      by aptitude or tricks
      by sleep's enormous fugue
      by his mother taking him on a fair sunny day
    through the ancient park
        with its statue of czarist Russia
      or his father dying
    on the wrong side of Jerusalem

Heavily now a man of more than golden years
    he lifts one foot then the other toward
    the next Halley's comet
his lifeline broken into many abstract chunks

      He stares at his dry corroded tongue
    at the unfashionable map of his cheeks
      into his eyes' barely detectable rivulets of moss
    at his teeth which remind him of baby marshmallows
and refuses to be the victim
of his own heroic life

    He turns away from the face of the moon
      that old sunscarred pug
      that looking glass no breath stirs with dew
toward summer's pilgrimage alone
    along the tawny heatlines heartdrawn
        The pen in sweet humor spells its sand

POINTING TO A BLACKBIRD

Arms breast-high bent at elbows
fingers drooping down
                    like leaves from an unwatered tree
            what does he bless
                        stern-faced
                        eyeholes black
                        unseeing
            father, whom do you bless?
        Surely not me who have with you
                    only the meaning of mechanical birds
                            clacking above in the city's marginal heaven

                    You left behind a dozen rusty needles
            instead of eggs
                        instead of a lighted candle
Even you must have had a woman
        somewhere on your tongue
                        or the alphabet of olives
                        or a knife's pure whisper

        Father with owls in his fingers prays
for a kind word
                from the oracle of orts
                the toothless beginning of eternity

    Or my other view
                    the bluebird nourishing the treelimb
                    as I look down from the mountains above Taos
                        that bluebird

I point to
am able to point to
as lovely in itself
no reference otherwise
secreting

A Good Story

This old and moderate desire for narrative
reminds me of autumn
                     of a drive we took through Bandelier's turning leaves
              scarlet, fierce gold and some still green
          also those black denuded poles
               shafts of a fire distant in time
               harrowing still the high ground on the way south
                   via Los Alamos
                     where everyone wears an image and a name
              Afterwards, continuing on
        we came through the mounds and mesas of Jemez clay
as violently red as the leaves
           and the sun that accompanied us
             as hotly gold as the earlier aspen
              of this fall we rode upon
           as if it were some perfect direction
        with a firm result
          I know this was not so
The purpose of our way merely intersected
          a certain hour of the season's best light
              What story
         can be told of it then
      of leaves and earth?
              No story but nostalgia
           a weakness of the eye which hordes
            its names and images
          of the ear which listens raptly to the eye
         and of the other senses
              their taste for a scent of clarity

in whatever they read as they act
A good story flows across the air piecemeal
the smoke of trees
the smoke of trees
The weather hurtling toward us
flings one dry crow after another into the cages
where our words pace back and forth
wild
cursed by day and by night
lulled to silence only by fresh red meat

THE INDIAN CAPITAL OF THE WORLD

In Gallup, in the Pizza Hut
    they go from table to table
        the sky behind them
    always tomato red
                  they carry this sky
        through the smoke of their very white cigarettes
    the fumes the clouds
                which need a location
  such as the sunspots in their eyes
    when they hold before the patrons
    a pair of silver earrings
           or a turquoise bracelet
It's a long way to Gallup from anywhere
    the light after snow falls differently there
           the owl's last incision, the truth's
             first question
  and they offer no solutions
        no revenge no whispering disease
Cheap jewelry and a thin crust of laughter
sometimes dark sunglasses
  sometimes a sky that topples to earth
    heavily
      thick in buffalo dust

MAN ASLEEP

Asleep at the wedge where wall joins wall
        wrapped in a blanket
overhead an airplane infinitesimal as a fly
          hums in a straight line
              that gradually fades into a point
                  finite

        only in retrospect
      while asleep against the wall
                  the man of science

        mutters in patches
      words we cannot understand
because they are numbers occurring in a dream
          equations perhaps
      that would embrace the airplane's arrival, departure
and all other trajectories of matter
             into a single kiss
                  a moment
             never abandoned
        a sound solid in the graph of time
        and also unavoidable as myth

      The square root of a tree
is the wall against which he sleeps
      altogether an order of dots and curvy dashes
          that would resolve
      in enduring love
if that were possible
if the world did not vanish in sleep

EMBRACE IN AN OPEN FIELD

They stand in a field
under a yellowish light
inseparable
a single figure
Days will pass and they will not move
and those who go by will wonder
at so humanly sentimental a statue

They embrace under the same yellowish light
not of the sun
rather of more tedious consistency
of the same texture as their lips
longing to part
but unable to
as the light also
would change
if it could
Years later the motorists who go by and see them from a distance
say, speaking through the glue of their individual tongues:
This is boring
They should be torn apart
Are they alive?

Eventually the light does rot like a dead lemon
the man the woman
grow differently get a divorce
and someone who doesn't see them any more
someone who wished them bad news
now yearns again

for that wintry light
their darker shape there in the field
formed as humans are

of blood, music and luminous air

EROTIC WOMAN

This is what I like about her: that she
thoughtlessly spreads her body across
whatever plan of earth receives her
and lies still   a lake
seemingly unruffled by wind
or the silent amplitude of her needs
If then she is a circle of water
if she is too prone to reside for long
in the harrowing streets
may a sailboat glide through her blood
a child's easy answer
to the problem of April and May
when the sun is still too alone:
a soft body in a gathering paradise

What I like about her: that she
does not awake with dirt on her face
with trembling legs and heart stuffed inside her sex
She will go out into the sounds
of cicadas and glassy buildings
will mingle with shopkeepers
on the classical shore
of her private ghosts   and not too quickly
open her purse
During the immense hours   daylight of dolphins and horses
she will meet strangers with her body
friends also   and with a spirit thoroughly large
encompassing reason as well as appetite
When she spreads her eyes her mouth

across the loud seclusion of another's

pantomime

her offering is not excessive

I like this about her: that she
wears her presence with a careless prescience
not wanting death but already storing it up
giving herself away
to the man in the drinking place
the woman behind the counter
Still, she holds herself implicit
her mind unclassified by strict space
in this or that barbedwire acre of weed or water
She thinks of pain
as someone she can call to
as a service of the spirit
and will not let go of her slender death
no matter how willingly she and anyone
obey her body's law

3
A Lover's Quarrel With America

THE CATERPILLAR

As they stand on the threshold
his mouth senses
the whirring inside her body
electric
wirelike
something coiled, captive
struggling to emerge
perhaps as word
or cry
and this conflict or perhaps a wound that still hurt
as it entered her tongue
reminds him of a surrogate birth
an upward spiraling along her spinal column
the caterpillar
vagina through uterus   womb
caught in her throat
cracking open
so that when they pause
to open their eyes
a blue butterfly
issues from her lips
disappears with one willowy moan
into abstract happiness
the universe of butterflies

CERAMIST

As she drinks the liquid from the soft cup
        her tongue enters an unlit corridor
        humid as the earliest moment she can recall
a blue flame a liquid flame
        Her mood melds into the cup's handle
        her mind a clay vessel
                containing shadowy milk

        She holds a woman's breast
                cupping the flesh towards her mouth
            Her tongue sucks the length of its memory
        the long-ago liquid
which her eyes have never called by its name
She washes the cup from her feelings
    body languorous from immersion
        mind thoughtful within a capsule of sleep
            so that she drifts entirely
    in a bath
of her father's semen
        swallowing swallowing
    in order not to drown

ANDROGYNE IN ALEPH

Speaks in a voice difficult with arranged symmetries
      to behead the gloved tulip of gender
      as if to be alone in a single self
         required too many curves of geometry
Alludes to concentric pools
         fishless
      warm under a sun that never lingers
    in the frozen zones
         If she calls herself "she"
    it is as choice
of one body against another
        or with
        To doubt but double
     as in couple
    Leans into her future braced only by light poles
    into which and around her body winds
      vine embracing
Dreams, fluid, flood
      bodysap translucent spilling down her thighs
        eyes tremble like water rippling
         after the cast stone
    Dream and dream parallel whatever she says
      lover lover
         curves her back backwards
     feet on grass hands touch sand
The black poll of her sex rises, curious, through the fevered white leaf

PHANTOMS AND ECHOES

                                        She suffers her monogamy
                        with bruising intensity and a sly
                                offering of her body to the imagination
                of imagined lovers
                        Many days pass ineptly
        forgotten in the oven   so black and spoiled
                                they break in her hands between
                                        one lust and the next

                        So the good skin of her face
                betrays a lost solitude
        (but not the husband not the children)
        her sleep so dense with dryads and lovers
                                that even awake they brush against her temple
                        warm her cheeks with long tongues
                In hiding from these phantoms
                        she covers herself with leaves
                                                lingers too often
                                among humans as chaste with her soul-making
                                as the squash and tomatoes she grows

        At forty she had become her self-portrait
                        fully approved by the academy
                                which is one of her acquaintances
                                never asking why her eyes
                        leak like cheap dye from their sockets
        why her mouth circles around itself hour after hour
                Yet her dreams say "There is a way
                A way
                        Away"

Again she visits her old photographs   those lovely gypsies
      who know a grammar
      through the forbidden echoes and pools
         And then again it is time to go home
                time to close the book

SEVERAL DESCRIPTIONS OF THEIR LIFE TOGETHER

His arm around her shoulder
    their heads touching as they huddle together
            We see the seams running down
      their backs
   and nothing else
           Next she is sitting in a deep chair
         legs crossed
     wearing red sandals
             only a caterpillar of pubic hair visible
  And he kneels at the juncture of two roads
hitching a ride
        blue backpack on the ground beside him
  Afterwards they jog together
     across hilly grass
           fog coming in from the ocean ahead
      so that we imagine them
     vanishing in the water
     nakedly taken, sweating hearts beating hard

Finally we do not see her face
    only the black hair streaming down
      as she hangs in air
          arms spreadeagled
      legs dangling
    in some formal posture of sleep
  he stretched out flat
bareassed
     on tough brown earth
     head cradled in his arms
  beside him a jug
       that gleams under the furrowing moon

In the Desert Alone at Night

He hunkers before the fire
clarifying himself by way of
   his perception of it
      as a microscopic shadow
        of the sun
     although it is night
    The fire is
all there is of voice
   out there amid saguaro sage and juniper
      whose origin could not be of the sun's law
        but rather of those aleatory upheavals
     which grow out of season
  and not according to steady graphs

So the fire kindles, cradles his gaze
   He rocks back and forth on his haunches
  occasionally casting more sticks on the flame
     keeping it going
       as if his mind
    depended on it
  as it does
the stars reaching down
   steadily reaching down
       to pull him up
     into their dense and charted communities

A stubborn man who squats
    to keep himself a matter of earth
       to leave the scrub of his name warm

View of the Riders

On horses single file
accompanied by slow violet shadows in sand and scrub
shadows like puddles of water irrigating fertile cropland
as I see them from behind
They head toward mountains
beige far before them
they themselves virtually black shapes in
the lateness
Horses and their riders hunching over
with only thin pale glints of sun steady on their shoulders
as if even these angles of light formed
but another aspect of their burden
I am not sure where they are going or why
only that the mountains
curve around them to the west
a slightly slyly darkening mass of beige
curve around them so voluminously so blankly
that the riders
as they wend forward
are suddenly   for a second   caught motionless in the falling away
of great heights
there on the rim of their odyssey   there at the abyss

A Lover's Quarrel with America

Reasonable as gray flowers
in the valley of mushrooms
impeccable as a soft whiskey entering the spine
on spiderlegs
                        the history of America
            spoils in its valise
left in some bus-terminal locker

                        Lacy brutal snow covers
                the harbor statue
                                    even in July
            Schoolbooks remind us of sucked-out pomegranates
    and buffalo bones lying stacked
in bosses' vaults
            in khaki thinking
                        and lazy bedrooms

                        Talking about America the hero
                opens his lips
        like *Hustler* pussy
He sprinkles green salt on his hair
            edges away from another discourse on cranky furniture
                        on bullfights and bearhugs
America he says is a platonic idea
                        a lens and a shadow
                        a white turd in the grass
I love America he says
        like Baudelaire loved his whore
                        with lime on his breath
                        with a musical aphasia in his brain

4
TELLING THE STORY

REVOLUTION

That horse comes toward us as always
at a slow walk
its rider swaying only slightly forward and back
as if in prayer
How hot it is!
and the horse's advance so slow
we are not sure of being there, somewhat living
should it arrive
Black hat black shadows around his eyes
the rider has been in that same saddle
for hundreds of years
starting from that one moment
when we all realized
that Death is a huge word
and that we ought to hear it everywhere
This *camposanto* or another
who cares

Suddenly the rider's bleached eyes
enter our hearts as always
and we know
the masters will never offer us
more than a grain of life
more than a taste of water
not even a strawberry
from the *norteamericanos* nor even a decent bullet
from the rider's saddlebag
We see once more and still more
how slowly the horse approaches

how rigid the hand that holds the reins
we are condemned to wait wait wait   to wait
and still to wait

SOMETHING SCHOEN & BERGIAN

All the mosquitoes must be revised
especially those in the interior of Florida
                              where the young Englishman came
              to eat oranges
          Later his score for the suite "Florida Oranges"
          arrived from the printer covered with bumps
which could not be erased
          "This awkward Braille is uncurable" he told his wife
before sitting down to compose another music
                                        without mosquitoes

          But back in Liverpool the workingman's town
                        inspiration was lacking
          He tore up his notes and waited for music to come   quite correct
buzzing from the bogs
                    "My mind is too smooth   I feel
                              like a window-cleaner"
                    he told his wife
      "spraying the universe with diminishing dice"
"Round orange oranges" she said
                                        and he believed her

EMERGENCE

Golden sand along the shoreline
                    a single figure stares out into the sea
                        almost black against
                        penetrating sight
            The figure does not move
        a pillar in the sand
        a luminous archive
                    mediating between sky and water
The littoral a membrane
                through which solitary mind
                        bedazzled by golden sand
                thinking louder than the waves
            contains its idea of mundo
                    its black transparency
            in the solar glass

            This figure sleeps under the pale sky receding
        a trace in the sand
                    memory flinging off water
                        to shape a voice
                            which at night screams out
                the shattered beauty of a peacock

Gulls fly in at dawn
        over wet kelp strewn in the sand
                    over the being that emerges once more
            eyes glittering
                        from the mother's angry hold

'THE PROBLEM OF INDIVIDUAL IDENTITY
IS THE DILEMMA OF PHILOSOPHY'

Silver-haired slender
                              he slipped into the pool
              naked alone among the other guests
                              He swam towards himself
                                                            or away
                        Ask then what his crime was
              that he must decide between
his body, solid, in the pool
              and the abstract heat in his groin

                              Brazen, the old man afterwards slithered
                                    onto the shelf the concrete slab
                                    from which daubs of grass
                                    and little dandelions sprouted
                                          his wet body
                              shining
              his armored gown
                              in the sunny slant
even his long slim cock
                        symbolic

              After he dressed
                        no one knew him
                        except by name
                              or as the old man who swam away
                        and left only his wet feet
              to shadow his going

back

into his nameless crime
            Ask then who he was
                among the other guests
                showing himself so naked
                almost invisible
        A mere sketch
inside the man's body he wore

ALGORITHM

"A romance with
the material must be well under way" before life begins
its lonely trust in another form
The language of Pascal is the sum of its odds
so that God varies in value
as metaphor in prosody accentuates
the similarities of things otherwise altogether unlike
When one's life so longingly loops around the older parts
of the brain
which know what to say but not how
the program begins itself
Anxiety in these terms is not the self's influence
rather it is the environment
which turns thought away from "repetitious aggregations of concrete instances"
toward "a single abstract insight"
The artificially intelligent human
corresponds to a flow/a flaw in the sequence of whatever river
is precisely like itself but never is

When I say I am anxious
I mean I do not live my life enough
am afraid of lacking the sum of my parts
Numbers are safer than sounds but harder to read
What answer am I to anybody's question?
"Chaos is captured in law"
But not God's who we learn
must remain one integer among many
Whose law then?

Of words
and the reader's interpretation of words
someone said I wouldn't bet on it

TELLING THE STORY
(for William Dowling)

Someone should tell the story
        of the lovely young woman who at nightfall
    leaves on her doorstep
    a little glass of red wine
        which in the morning she pours out on the few
                    chrysanthemums
      that grow beside the house
            She lives intransigently alone
       in a forest
      where no other creatures exist
             not even bugs
     No one knows where she gets the food that sustains her
   or, more significantly, the wine
Why does she have no lovers?

      She exists as a solitary instance
   of human law under a sun that snips
     disturbing euclids from the axioms of her surroundings
   We may imagine then how longingly
        she fears
      the unexpected footstep
   someone   a sorcerer perhaps
or a simple man wearing mudclotted boots
a bear possibly   its shaggy embrace already sketched in
     by a big-city artist
   who will dominate her night
   She fears the enclosure of her dreams
by the dreams of another one

circle within circle
surrounded by an infinity of concentricities
                In that superbly ingenuous way of hers
the lovely young woman contrived a geography
distinct from history
               like a Sleeping Beauty who killed her sleep
               and does not wish to wake
                    among sweaty pascals which read out
               ancient moralities of the heart
        In her forest alone
she remains indomitably loverless
What we don't know
        (can only guess as storytellers do)
is that each nightfall's glass of wine
                  is lovingly
                    in loneliness
                  poisoned

DILEMMA OF MEANING

Nothing is more conclusive
than these objects
                    as they look at him
          as he takes them in   disguises them
                    to look like he does
                              None of them means what he says
                              in describing them to his sister-in-law
                                        who believes him
                                   as she does her mandolin
          an instrument so gently moving
it carries him toward the greenest fields the bluest bay

                         The objects on his bedroom wall
               the house's furniture
                              are problems much like dice
                                   whose spots are restless
                    or his sister-in-law's
               long bare legs

                         Brother's wife
                                        marathon runner
          one of those human objects whose patience exhausts itself
               the subjunctive relationship
                    without fringes
                              Reason can go no further
                         it cannot fall to the ground
So then, the essential excerpt
                    So then, always room for his tongue
                         in the mandolin's mouth

always a minor joy
in what he cannot possess
possessing him

There is No Reason to It

She expresses outrage
at so much verbal texture
                    in his heart
It offends her simplest desires
        her hope of a transcendent voyage with him
    to the stars and beyond the stars
                their mutual solitude
                    a form of transcription
        closer to collage
                            than all his words
                            which are closed networks
                            of allegiance
                            what is now called
                    classical modernism

                She stops
            a worried moment shading her brows
    then understands herself speaking
                                    in clumps
                        hard clumps
                It is the times she says
                The days are stitched together
                        with gray thread
        and his heart is now painted glass
All right then
she will be his object
let him pour his deadly formulations
                        into her ear
        let him display her

84

on his dirty finicky pages

> her own words by now
> stacked together
> like leaves the leaves of an artichoke
> green destinies that cannot breathe

DIVAGATION FROM A LINE IN *The Aeneid*

"Old age in the gods is green"
            not however the ivy that hugs the backs
        of New England churches
               or moss clinging to the boles of moist sunless oaks
        Green perfectly nocturnal
inhabits the edges of forgotten customs
               and witnesses the girl's rape by her father
             Green preserves ideas
        in cultural bottles
                       and regards every morning
                       with a powdery gaze
             When gods grow brittle in their towering glass
        they return to their sources in slow pools
        moonpetals afloat fresh in the water
where green freezes moment by moment
        where green disengages
from truth
        and emerges armed with wily music

                     Gods in their great age
           do not protect
           do not reveal
They are stealthy in sex
                    and ruthless
              Their thought grips the human heart
        with monotonous endurance
             within little frames of iron, gilded
In old age the gods see through green eyes
        Green accompanies their departure into the shadows where
             furious trumpets greet them

Saying is Believing

Dull afternoons when you look for something visual
when the air gathers moss before it gets to your lungs
when even God is a thought
            you sleep like the brown fedora
                  pulled far down over the fat man's forehead
                and when you wake
          a stuffed hummingbird sticks to your tongue
          trying to lift off with all its meager memory

Sometime soon luck will be stronger than many bad mistakes
        You put on a gray double-breasted suit
        with a white hankie sprouting from the pocket
              go out to prowl for the enemy
              Saying is believing
     it says on the tape
this is a movie nobody ever made

New Poems
1997

I
A Candle

UNCLE HYMIE

My Uncle Hymie
cracked his head in Friedrichstadt
and became a natural surrealist.
He would visit us
in the Bronx
and leave a memory
of his presence,
a circle in a Rubik's cube,
a picture no one could recognize.
The last time I saw him
he was wearing a tan suit,
well-pressed,
and a subtle
blue-and-gold tie
pinned to his light-blue shirt
by a rearing silver horse.
Hymie was one of my mother's brothers,
Sam's twin.
He had fallen from a barnloft
when they were three.
Later Sam got married,
became a sculptor,
mostly animals,
while Hymie sold
ladies' foundation garments.
Sometimes it was hard to believe he wasn't right,
but when that last time
he took off his jacket, his tie, shirt, and trousers
to show us the corset he was wearing,

my mother placed a hand
over my young eyes
and told Hymie to behave himself.
I remember this, how this uncle
became my favorite
among four others.

EXPECTING ME

I would greet myself zealously,
suspecting I might forget to arrive
            and lie in the water,
                        dreaming.
                Mother and father,
                    buried
        in Congregation Beth Israel's cemetery,
would they know me
                    now that I have grown older
                and find less humor in nature?

        The feast is held on Sunday
after an ordinary Sabbath.
I keep expecting myself — the food smells
                        like angels.
                I have noticed
                great crowds swarming
            through the sunlight.
Experimentally, I touch where my heart
                    should be.
        I am deserted inside myself.
        I realize that life is exaggerated.

Have I come alone or with others?
        My parents, I know, expect me
as if I were Elijah
                    come to collect his respect
                    from the Passover dinner.
            I have never seen him

even though my father
hid the matzoh under his pillowed seat
                              every time.

            I will come, having lived with
                    the worms.   My eyes
                    will be powdered with dust.
        Still, I will know my name
and welcome the presence that lives
                              on Earth
                    whatever his faith might lack.
        I will grow
into myself like a flower from its precept.
The best news reveals itself in cycles.
                    I have wandered far
into the thick horizon where no Hebrews live.
I am ready to return to myself,
the one who expects Lazarus in the mail.

THE FAMILY

Lydia, my one wife,
told me if I took Bly to Santa Fe
that day
I should move out.
The children were up at the usual time,
a Saturday.
It was the last day of our family.

I found a hovel backed on
an alley
in the student ghetto
and stayed there.
Why was she my wife?
The children went with her back to the coast
to a temporary exile, though the pictures
that took their lives then
are not faded even today.

The mind is abstract and emotional.
Madness divines the secret of ellipsis,
acts surely on the evidence of voices
fed through a straw
to the brain's
deceiving motives. Or was it the blood
gone sour
before the will could lock into
its adulthood?

Lydia as a mother could not become then
what I'd hoped for her,

                    a reason against her slavery
          to the moon's dark god.
          I took away Celena and Paul.
               I had earned them
through a pitiful inversion of the wound Lydia
took long before, in the paintings her youth
once promised. Even later, in Venice West,
                    she'd sketched with skill
a man's genitals
                         and significant birds.

We three came to the garage she'd rented
                              for her work
          and we shared the spoils.
As Paul said,
          we were scavenging a life.
Where does love go during death?

IF SHE WEREN'T SO OBSESSED

Aboard the aircraft
heading home,
the woman seated beside me
tells me she is going to
her lover
in Gallup,
which I know is the Indian Capital of the world.
I have the window seat
coming from LAX.
In front another
window seat
empties.
She is attractive, obsessive,
reading Whitman, one eye on that seat.
I can see her in the tape
I am making, in my eyes.
If she is so dangling
how well does her lover
steady her, provide safety and a home
after she flies every weekend to Albuquerque
where he picks her up?
He is not
Indian
but also reads
Whitman
and even Joy Harjo.
I tell her I taught
Leaves of Grass in a class at Hawaii-Manoa,
but she is too obsessive to wonder why
this matters. She tells me

she works at Occidental
                              Insurance
in LA, not "selling" but "advertising."
                              My tape is rolling
                    even as I watch her
                                        get up
and move to the seat in front of me.
            I can barely see
her dark hair
                    from a side angle.
If she weren't so obsessed I could have
            eased her into some sly comfort.
            The voice in my eyes repeats
                                        the words
                    it has learned
in describing her to myself. When we land,
she rushes to the front,
                    not even looking at me.
My eyes freeze her
in the frame when I stop recording,
and curiously edge toward her lover, too:
                    who waits like a taxi,
            his meter
                    running.

CHRONIC

I love you deliberately
as if it were on order
from the commanding officer of my helplessness,
and I am swimming
in your future.
You say your mind is set
on automatic impulse,
on the eloquence of body.
Wherever I go the feeling
of disruption
itemizes what I would say to you.

How little you forget in my words'
confusion,
when I reply
to the distance
I hold in my arms
as if it were you.
Yet love is not an industry,
and if I use
frightening language
I mean it
to be
no less than my confession.
How terrible this sounds:
could I be speaking
in my reasonable Jewish way,
you listening with Irish eyes
smiling sadly?

There must be this illness
                          between us,
                          the chronic pain
            you cannot share,
        the chronic fatigue.
My birth reads from right to left,
            revealing a difference in logic:
                mine green but static,
                yours as the seasons go.

Your blue eyes commit me to limits
set in bronze, a medallion of sorts.
        The gleam follows me
                as I move,
                              implicated
                in a simple love
            that goes nowhere.
The image of your legs in black
                              spike heels
        is true as only time is true
        when it stops. Then the sunlight
is someone else's, for whom you wait
                speaking through your pain
            into mine.

MY GINSBERG POEM

The day after Allen Ginsberg's death,
I notice the hole where I sat or stood
or lay on my back. This is complicated by the exterior
that reclines into salt, near stunned simplicity.
He talked of Buddha, a friend in the listening dark
where anyone may hear the alphabet consoling

from aleph to omega. Some letters are never enough,
merely duplicating speech. Yet he wrote more feelingly
than friendship could suppose, for he was words'
doctor, to be lamented by all who can remember
his vision of time, the chance we all take.
He was in a sense selfless. As if he could be more

than the wish of himself. And he was. A friend's
friend. Holy the howl inside the mouth that alters
the century with lyric, satiric force,
a comet dwindling in space. Such is the dew
spread over the heart, one of the feminine angels
we have never heard of. He spoke in trust of spectral

music without solemnity, King and song of May,
who hustled wisdom along the streets everywhere, teacher
of more than grace. I who denied the dog in myself,
who repressed the illusions that brought me here
to this American desert, I sweep the dust of my bones
through the stones' window, thereby to configure

his voice as metaphor of Earth. Simple is not always
easy, the records show. Distillation equals a variety

of laughter, foam in the laundry basket, quick sizzles
apropos of this April when the rivers overflow.
Allen, rest in your sphere of sun, the gamble won.
Be thou, as you might say, the grizzled wonder

of our poetry, always youth among the ages and crucible
wherein we boil our words clean. Bring us back
to the flowers' multitude and the droppings of our digestion.
I rehearse this question you ask me without
meaning to. I flash through your naked hospitality
as one who never knew you well, but knew enough to want

to be kind in your reflection, and now reflect again
how your travels brought me home. Language
was your rough spot, the broom that left the world
with dignity, even as it spattered the air,
a fevered shower. You are already classic, definitive.
I thumb a ride on the road of your death.

My Parents' China

Having been born Orthodox
                         and asthmatic,
            I marked the marching
                  tin soldiers
from the beginning of time. My chaplain
            was not kosher. He had a blue
                              beard
that the army allowed him to keep,
                        my army.
            We lived on the fourth floor
where my mother daily dusted the wax fruit
in a porcelain bowl. I was accompanied
by aunts and uncles, the breathing
                        of an ox
         pulling the entire army.
                  I was ashamed of being
                        a Jew.
            My father and mother
could not command my faith
except in silent films, their voices
            resonant of early shtetl communities,
                        Baltic villages.
            I did not fit in once I learned
                        English.
            I've always straggled
                  as if to follow
was my only hope.
Then, I rubbed against metaphysics
         to believe if I could

In a God not military
                    but anxious.

Who was I to manufacture fruit
        for a black, polished table?
        Or silver—maybe a wedding gift—
        or dishes orange-and-white
                            bone china?
These colors repeat themselves
                like a platoon,
        marching, marching into fire.
                    British redcoats maybe
                        falling like apples
in that remote garden where I gasped
for my mind, never believing
                as far as I remember.
                We all died
        as stereotypes of poor Jews
in silence, bearing no arms,
                            begging alms
            from aunts and uncles.

        If I came back from the dead
it was because I learned English,
                            right there
                in the Bronx.
I still feel cordoned off,
inhabiting a nevertheless glistening
                            island.
            I confess, I confess

in a parody of the confessional,
                the paradox
                        of belonging
        to a bridge of scholars
who mark time through the history
                        of the aleph.
                I continue almost groundless,
                hoping for a thought
        that would release
        my mad, dead wife,
all other raped and murdered wives,
also men who sweated in their beds,
so I could swear on anyone's Bible,
                chant my bar mitzvah song
                        for life,
always life amid the polished brass.
        Even though I relax now,
                lacking Jehovah even more,
Jewish in complications,
Jewish in my ancient tribe, whoever they are.

MATH TEACHER

Perces Witt, who in her late 50s
                lived with her mother,
taught Geometry and Trig
at Belmont High,
where I became editor of the school paper.
She spoke mildly and graded fairly,
             believing perhaps that she was
                   content
          in what her life
          had chosen for her
        and that the grades she gave
were evidence of that positive curve.
I understood along the way that once
she had been on the stage, had married
                the manager
       of her dance troupe,
     who beat her up often enough
so that it wasn't long before she got a divorce.
     She went to college in Indiana,
         earned a degree.
     She'd given up dancing at that time,
and men.   I could see that her legs
              were still fine,
the sort of thing that I'd begun
        to think about seriously.
     I learned these things about her
from my Journalism teacher,
who was her companion sometimes,
and possibly would move in with her later

if her mother died.
        I don't know why
she told me all that
           since I couldn't write it up
     for the paper anyhow.

COMING HOME

It was during a summer
                in Buffalo
        that I discovered I had an allergy
           to mold.
A sewer smell ran by outside the house
I was living in.
        The sludge must have infected
                  the house.
         I was teaching at SUNY
             that summer, during which
my son turned 13.
                No bar mitzvah though.
        I was too busy
breathing hard, a heavy wedge in my chest,
and thinking about my preps, the scene,
                and my students.
      Driving back to Albuquerque,
        I felt like a normal sick person,
           but soon,
        back in the house I rented,
the allergy returned, driving me
              from my room
       to another
and another until I had to move.
        I bought a house
where the allergy gradually weakened
        and left me alone,
though my older books are still infected.

I don't know if God followed me home,
                    as the mold did,
from that forgotten bar mitzvah,
            but I think so
            in my superstitious moments.
My son is married now, has two children.
Maybe I have repented: I see
            a candle in my breathing.

II
Surprises Even Gravity

Brushing Up

To do it again
to rehearse doing it again
I read prose poems by a woman
who refers persistently to her cock
and to lovers
with whom she uses it
Then too
I look at Motherwell's
collages
which remind me of Diebenkorn's
oils and works on paper
although they are dissimilar
There are these connections
which if I could do it again
would solve the question
of why I think in long terms when they are
really short

To believe in one's power
is to forget
the tubers in the ground
dying
I burgeon from that intimacy
somehow still forming
through whispers   still
lodgers
among the mind's cold furnaces
And the woman who compels
the pain her lovers bestow on her

becomes the destiny of a deep red
dildo

I regret being so modest
                barely knowing how to do it
                            to get it done
                as Diebenkorn-Motherwell did it
        and Gorky in the pastures where his youth
        drove him to be united
                with tall grass
I would munch hay if only
a single word of mine could satisfy
                            that woman
                            who moans
                            so successfully
                            in circles
                            alone in her lovers

            But if I could paint
I would grow inside my heart like a patient
                            fig tree
        older in daring   visual as blue
                            mists
                    I can't wish for
    resentment as I scheme to desire again
        as though this could never become
My mind is lost in her compilations of despair
Yet she demands respect for being a master of love
            persistent in submitting to pain
as if it were the laurel crown at last

I do what I do more often than I think
The secret is not to think about it
                              but to wait
with ordinary surprise   envision the oils
                              and acrylics
                              of Frankenthaler

                 References intuit fresh power
            somewhere the inner world releases
            and goes on doing so   a wet paintbrush
                 licking at completion

MIND AND MAZE

Forgetting whom the dream favored
can be crucial   Existence lies in wait
                              to corrupt
                  what was never soiled
                        in the mouth
          and the same could be said
                  of Barnie's Beanery
            where the artists gathered
to talk it over   to assess marginal and
                          vivid confusion
                  But the dream too
                        asserts its art
                        as a favor
          to the woman with tan
                        solid thighs
          who sits down at a nearby table
smiles readily as if to ask for instructions
          The soul is ready to swell to the top
          where only the average mood prevails
                These are all tricks
          of the collapsible trade
that anyone can learn with frugal intensity
                She in her beautiful way
                orders a plate of luxury
          The mouth decides to grow infinite
And where are those lectures on
                        Las Meninas
                that drove the students
                        to all their mirrors?

It was an eating place in LA
the woman an inverted idea
A casualty of the dream
The soul has fled   incapable of adjusting
                         to this society
                    the mind a maze
                    where thoughts follow
                         rainbows in the night
Too much pollution exaggerates the effort
to acquire dimension   A toothless widower
                         thinks he's a romantic
                    whose line is broken up by
                         crests and windfalls
then an abstract drumroll
                    The attractive well-formed woman
                         leaves secretly
The landscape vanishes   I am invisible
                    to myself
So much to do   so much to-do
everyone so dramatic about a game of leapfrog
                    Old cowboy paintings in the attic
                    Long ago the world wanted us

BRAINWORK

Still the brain writes   the still
brain writes   records itself
        as if on a visionary island
                beyond thought   The voice
                redirected by electronic
                        whispers
                  guides itself
            by oars or
whatever comes to hand   which is a replay
of thought   a gray moon
                    responding to moral
                      incursions

The brain is a carpetbag
everyone a story   impulses one
                    gathers together
        or affixes
      to expected terms

      Mind satisfies brain energy
as if to agree that computers are simple
        in the sort of direction
          that accumulates knowledge
            stuff and nonsense
        To be actual
    stimulates comparisons
all the vital fluids accept in flow
Ill-fitting synapses cross introvert sensations
                palliate

what comes through
the soapy water
as a tributary cutting-edge

A businessman's thinking arranges the brain
in a meter-field
plus value negative
as regards the transformation
of one's endorphins   Please be beautiful
the computer says
a brain of its own

Space wrinkles near black holes
the pull
surprises even gravity
when time disappears
perhaps hides in a sublime
intelligence
So thorough is the fascination
with those special muscles
of love that a time comes
when lips
suck up everything
in the way a good ear
completes sound

In its mass
life is formless   What can be said
regards the brain's body
as an opportunity to shape

the transmission of affect
                    Later the gray moon
                              shifts to a green way
                It's all in the shaping
how vision argues for the body's feedback
                    amid evanescence
the time of our lives

SAIDLESS

Quotation marks   stand tall   alone
nothing between them   The voice
     which could speak
     empties itself of sound
       so that nothing could write
     even a sonnet
quoting Shakespeare
         The tongue exasperates

   thick

        stuck

    in dry saliva
Who could then reciprocate what
        remains

    hidden in the pen?
Nothing is a blindfold
The eye stares into capture

Praise can be earned only for excess
for what in form betrays by less
      than the kept
       oracle
   Eyes abandon the voice
in quotation marks so that nothing
    can enter
whatever happens
      Quiet
    as in a pause
      continuing
    as a buzz in the phone

                    dry no answer
                            ever
To review in meditation all the words
                        that suffer,
        a complete xerox of events
        Simple bare quotation marks
        tell all that can be desired
from questions   This then that rests
            in the core of breath
            the speech appropriate
                    to silence

And as Jabes might have said
        the book is fully middle
        which accounts for the blindfold's
            gathering in
                of all entelechies
        the heart's womb
quoted in context   To read believes
                    in gratitude
            even if the signature is formless
Prophets wander through air
                    relaying messages
God waits as we do
            Earth moves page after page
            quoting its destiny

WAKING UP CHILLED

Yesterday the music said the sun
is a lonely system though certain in its
        fruit-giving and place
        among orbiting islands
            But comment on the sun
    is a lack of safekeeping
The human regards itself as a camera
               of the sun
        yet no one feasts
           regardless

        Humor waves its red cape
    to the heart of its fruition
as if an animal could laugh
    Who sees in its night
            a soul?
Quotient remains side-locked as glorious
           root
        of chicken-wire
    The world moves into range
    of the lens and all music
           whitens
    a rage
following ordinary mutations

Nothing is less hopeful
    than the wonderful nature
        objects have
as some kind of residue of human

                                        concern
Lines of limericks coincide
        with apertures
                                and the cold
                cry of lemons
        fallow in supernal
                                longings

Art is left to hang among the brides
who wait as anchors in what the eye
can no longer
                        remember   It is time to turn
        the sand-clock toward Sunday
        where the old woman knits
                        a sweater
                for the music
        that drifts through the little doors

Stevens might have said that fiction
        is an opportunist   considering
        that what is true
                        might never be thought
                        A photograph
                                enlarges
                the sun's departure
as if one could imagine a day
                during which there was no occasion
                A mood in the swing
of goldening leaves   the merchant
                                for once

                                    forgotten as a pin
                                        in the sleeve

            Mortality can be a fine thing
                            in the multiplying heft
                                    between arms and legs
                Who can be so right
            as to never leave off consuming edges?
                            Yet the slate narrows
            the pictures follow a totally black trend
            The sun too will commemorate its dirge
                    as wind speculates too freely
                            the remnant of its ego   Go to
                                    says the old woman
                                    knitting for time's dog
Do not define the superior epoch
                    no one relies any more
                                        on the rusty
                                            Grail

                If the olive dries
        in the sun's absolute
                        nothing can take away
                        the memorable taste
            The dark horse wins the corona
        Everything is original in its once again
        and how the drive begins in combustible air!
                        what is known conceals
                                        the happenstance
                Go then stranger whose voice apportions

Your curious skin embodies the woman
                    sprawled in a field
              alive or dead
  like the Black Dahlia torso severed
              from who she was
That is but one instance of gore and mystery
          and as God is the witness
                    death was no motive other than
              the incentive for waking up
                              chilled
                and quietly remorseless

SO MUCH WOMAN

In what has become feminism
            features of coagulate
                          mortality
           A woman
           designs her copula
           with lust for perfection
      Texturally life regrets its passing
but what woman would want to dream only of suggestion?
Reason is its own cause   the person it belongs to
                    admires the form of its love
But nowhere in feminism
        does complication resolve into neutrality
        which is why captivity   as a mode of address
                        completes a cycle
              Maybe women are not examples
                  as history expects them to be
        but are heard
        like raging bells in a sunny afternoon

Quietly who goes there if not acceptable   in principle
to the surplus every hour becomes?
                A woman applies
                   herself to being
                 recorded
            not in a bottle
        The exact witnessing
      explodes in golds of paint   to be stamped on the age
                     beauty's
             prime reversal

Anyone who moderates a conviction
realizes that face and body
need support from mythic order

The woman
I have in mind
speaks notably
of oppression
as of a summer
among the dry branches in men's eyes
their hands pumping the air
punching it   a woman between their eyes
This woman originates
breath   she breeds
words that crowd the air
with enough space to signify her evolution
She waits just outside the door
singular and protracted
Time is a lingering craft   used and using
This woman belongs to the vision
that I can see only in that blackness behind the weather
Who can believe in the version of a postcard?

WHAT MATTERS

It stalls   the music   says the man
who reads his litmus paper   as if no sound
                    in the courtyard could retaliate
                        He expects the day to settle
                                    into his womb
                        black sheep
                    that he is   Yet could anyone cite
a juster cause than comparing "compression is all"
to poetics that aspire to community
                    among races? He reads acid
all the headlines red   the brewery
                    north of his bench   brick red
                                    and who dares to come
                        bearing salt
                    and a devious station to the world?
                    We know that God
            is too convenient
                    an incitement to the longer shapes of time
blown out on the rocks
The will sustains flowers beaten by
black hail without remorse
                    The man who believes in diamonds
                    shares only what he lacks
                                    forensics in four senses

                    and the lack
presumes a music not yet forgotten   a bruise
                                    deep in the moon
What alters is the brain   not the thought
The man's hearing stalls as it glares into wickedness

We are not we   but others

What matters

is that everyone race together

the marathon on and on

Black man rigorous

in presuming the lemon-lit morning

includes his shade

Heaven exists somewhere in love's leftovers

Blood burns like oil   symmetrical

with its opposite

enduring the long haul

right   right on the ball

Rilke's Razor, Jung's Version

This razor is terrible   it fills the air
clinging   a triangle of mirror   as if we could
                            look into it
                            as it emerges
                    from the brown wooden box
        If we are frightened
                                    the angel
                        of archetypes
has shaped hope into an inlaid silhouette
                of the Venus de Milo
        to console us   it would appear
by slicing away our too-human shame

        Time is beautiful if we could
        share it with our lives   Who watches over us
                    so that we may believe in
        Rilke's angels?
        Is there a name to relieve us
                        of our loneliness
                    our fierce expectations?
        The razor is our name   we are brief
                            in happiness
                yet refer to it
        as a passenger we bear

        Our unconscious is the therapy
                            we lack
To be human reminds us that to define
        significance

                    is an obsession
                              too narrow
                    to see in the specular design
Our shame belongs to us
                              like a birthmark
                    We are in terror of beauty
          the maze that guides us
          out of our peripheries
where shadows move

                              prehistoric

                    Murder is the archetype
of our definition   our angel who yet plays
                                   upon our hope
                              We dissect in order to be healed
          of death's foreshadowing
Rilke   master of pain and the rosethorn
                              he bled away from
                    tells us we live in fear
                              of our eyes
that we must change our lives
or go blind in Venus' groves
          Yet he too smiled
for his countesses   lived in Schloss Duino
                              rent-free

          There is no closure
                    although to end needs us
frayed as we are by life   sometimes old
          or madly young   What good is beauty?

It is the good that freezes despair
                         in its mirror
               This homage
loves Rilke though his wife his daughter
               slept far from their share
                              of his life
He passed through
                         the razor anyhow
               and now murmurs in the box Mel
Chin found for him
so that we hear him still
               an answer in the mind of beauty

WAITING FOR THE CHILD

Forgive me if this that I know
is an old voice far from where I loiter
in this city waiting for
                    the child to summon me
The voice begins in a quiet synagogue
Hard to decide
            if it is singing or manipulating
            the air to change speeds   but it is safe
                    to gather into it
            I heard it first when the white owl
flew across my windshield   this in those days when I drove
that tomato-red Lincoln Town Car like any prince
                    quick in his blood
            and it was then a soprano flagrant in its ease
                            a comfort its triumph
                    Watching the road
                    I could almost hear the breeze
            whispering through my mind
a devotional air   something aspiring to peace

Lately I've taken to pressing God for another chance
though I'm not a criminal   I think now
                    only when it recovers
                            its voice
            My shoes rot in my thought
            wandering as I do between incense-candles
                    and auto graveyards
Where do I suppose I'm going when I go?
            Windblown chimes tinkle among the olive trees

Where I have come from
I'm a transient in prayer
believing I hold the universe in my blood

It will end in blasphemy   The voice will cease
my hands lie fallow on the riverbank   the child
will never come
                              The two tramps agonize over
                                        antagonize
                                        each other
                    More mercy in a cup of tea
                    than in all of piety
            The moment goes awry
        fulfilled only in its overflow

IDA

I see yesterday as if
                    it were tomorrow
the woman jogging   conscious only
                        of her body
                    moving through drifts
                    of departed weather
                    each stride
            a muscle to be overcome
She will run six miles   part of a marathon
                    others will begin and finish
            what Pheidippides timelessly ran
            cramped with victory

I know her I think   She is my father's lover
            I have lost track of my enemies
                    The woman   I name her Ida
                    who speaks
                from the Ozarks   soft slanted words
            Ida whom I first encountered
among Lee Friedlander's nudes
I couldn't see her face then as she lay
                        stomach down
on a couch   back buttocks thighs
            visible to the naked imagination

                    My father
                turned his back to the sound
            I thought of as my extraordinary wish
                to draw as well as he

Ida studied in Knoxville Tennessee
                    to be a doctor of kindness
taking in men and women as strays
feeding them
                    From her mind she extracted
          a Jewish ghost who was not hers   the name
          she identified to me
          ,   as burned in the camps
                              But she wasn't
                    a woman I could bring in from her past
as if she were a concession to the perfect alibi
          for which I wrote my exigencies

I handle my thoughts arguably as marbles
I would have lived in the Ozarks
                              if she brought me there
                                        a return
                    to her speech curving
                              doubling back like an arch

My father still draws his angels
          his deft hand reminding me of Ida
who has left a generous voice to take me through
                    the years' vortices
          Time lost is no time but the present
                    where she pretends to die
                              leaving me
          a segment of what she touched
                              wanting in me

Where is the living woman who arched her body
back in a sumptuous
regard of the silence
                    we invest in?   I have contoured
                                        Ida
                        as a willingness to assume
                        care of my ego

                    She loved women too I think
                    as I read into a story she wrote
            I study her direction
as a move toward the recuperation of the body
I left her in Tennessee years ago
                    I carry her with me
                                to the shadow of old age
                                        I take care
                                        of Ida
                        a story in photographs
                    staring at me
Time wanders in me   in Ida's creation
                    based on a few words taken at a party
But who is she   that woman jogging?

CORRECTING THE MOTION

We calculate the em's and en's with a ruler
or whoever is in charge   and thus delimit black
and white or yellow or orange
                    This is to change a design into systems
                        although that's old now
                                and words delight in securing
                                a graph for a documentary
                        Alone we or I access
                        the road ahead

To trim is not to compare   not to apologize
                                The mind shortens
                                        its voice
            How to resolve clarity
            becomes the kernel
of possible attitudes   Nowhere does the print
evoke a formula more colophonic than
                                    history would
                                    demand   We resist
                                    alternatives
                                only because virtue is painful
                                and fairness weak
                    Corporate windows glare
into the fly-man's eye   maybe an investment
                        in questions unanswerable   shaped
                    to find a home in bitter shadows

        Foreclosure adapts to the page like birds
delineate the air to predict the source of flight

                                        Not everyone
knows a radius that could equal what is most local
Reading is love in the corner there as corporate as *could be*

                              Arrival can be swift
                                        as those who have left
            do not return
                        Frequently nothing absorbs   the ink doesn't dry
            we hardly refine our hands
Or I exclude myself from the instant

                                        Publication denies holograms
                        as if one knew the name
                                        beforehand   The alternative
                                        to seduction
                        is removal of tar
                        from the voice promised
long before anything could be done

The short of it belongs to fame as required
                        among athletes of the main stream
                        of forgetfulness
Whatever fails to correct the motion
                        incorporates complexity
                        without the simple coherence the world expects
                                        from truth
                        The vanishing American
                        is nobody but a printed form
            I look like myself
only when somebody quotes me

UNDER DEPTH

And so there may be
nothing under
the depth
that anyone can invoke as subliminal to intention
Risen silence occurs
venturing farther than intended
To go back volunteers another depth   a past
figural in the emergence of insight
of the new
Two speakers converge
One into the other   meet in common ground
saying largely an opening into a crowd
but it can't be said that they know an optimal mood
heartening the heart
I understand their foreign language
without naming it   is this a dream?
How I got there matters only if I intended it
Depth under depth   I wallow in others
headless
a trouble spot
I would worship the name of my silence if this
would not demean it
I have gotten rich forgetting dreams
I forget my name in the book of reason
Who knows me wonders at the pyramid my life
has undergone   the chops in style   of gradation
as a blue motif   in what
I can't help
but see

refracted as dreams' modifier
If what is beneath the world is a verb how to raise it
so the act concurs with all the rules
inscribed by science in myth?
Usually blank words fill in
the occupied spaces I read among Hebrews
who remind me how esoterically I have quoted
the name
that lies recumbent in willows
I look but make out only myself
as heart in image   No more reclusion now
the fire wanes
I am one mood among all people and starve
for ashes in the silence of a vertical truth

COLOPHON

Typeface:: **Joanna**
designed by **Eric Gill** (1882-1940);
flat serifed, exhibiting robust bluntness with
certain eccentricities in its harmony of shapes
—"a" vs. "e", for example. *As well, the italic is an*
idiosyncratic example of a sloped roman, upright but narrowed,
darker, and offering an unusual "g". Named after his youngest
daughter, Joan, and made for HAGUE & GILL, the press
run in partnership with her husband René,
its first use was for Mr. Gill's book
An Essay on Typography (1931).

•

Book design by J. Bryan

Born in New York City, Gene Frumkin has spent by far the majority of his life in the West, first in Los Angeles and since 1966 in Albuquerque. After matriculating at UCLA, he became a journalist for 14 years before moving to New Mexico to take a position at the University of New Mexico. He is now Professor Emeritus of English at that institution.

Frumkin has published 11 books of poems, including three chapbooks. His poetry has appeared in *The Paris Review, Poetry, Sulfur, boundary 2, Tyuonyi, Hambone, Conjunctions, Manoa, Chelsea, Cafe Solo, The Evergreen Review, Choice, The Malahat Review,* and many others, as well as a variety of poetry anthologies, among them *¡Saludos!, New Mexico Poetry Rennaissance,* and *Voices from the Rio Grande.*

Frumkin has served as an editor of *Coastlines Literary Magazine, The California Quarterly, The San Marcos Review, The Blue Mesa Review, The New Mexico Quarterly,* and *The Indian Rio Grande: Recent Poems from 3 Cultures* (anthology).

He has accepted numerous literary awards that were never offered to him.